MW01048049

The Twelve Days of Christmas

The Twelve Days of Christmas

Morning and Evening Thoughts on
Immanuel: God with Us

Roger Ellsworth

Unless otherwise noted, Scripture quotations are taken from the New King James Version®. Copyright © 1982 by Thomas Nelson. Used by permission. All rights reserved.

Copyright © 2016, Roger Ellsworth

All rights reserved. No part of this book may be reproduced, scanned, or distributed in any printed or electronic form without permission.

This Edition: 2017

ISBN 978-0-9988812-0-1

20170423-NKJV-LS

Great Writing Publications
www.greatwriting.org
Taylors, SC
in partnership with
sermon**audio**.com

Table of Contents

About this Book

Christmas comes but once a year, so the old song goes. Why is this wonderful holiday celebrated and so loved all these years since the birth of Jesus?

Immanuel—meaning God with us—was born in obscurity, a humble birth that would probably have gone almost unnoticed unless angels had appeared to shepherds and brought the good news of his first advent.

What does this mean to us today? Find out more by reading and reflecting on these short, enjoyable devotions. Use them in the twelve days leading up to December 24th (two a day) or even read just one a day from December 1st, finishing up on the night before Christmas!

A Christmas Hymn

O come all ye faithful joyful and triumphant
O come ye, O come ye to Bethlehem;
Come and behold him born the King of angels;
O come let us adore Him,
O come let us adore Him,
O come let us adore Him, Christ the Lord.

God of God, Light of light
Lo, He abhors not the virgin's womb;
Very God begotten not created:
O come let us adore Him,
O come let us adore Him,
O come let us adore Him, Christ the Lord.

Sing choirs of angels, sing in exultation
Sing all ye citizens of heaven above;
Glory to God in the highest:
O come let us adore Him,
O come let us adore Him,
O come, let us adore Him, Christ the Lord

A Christmas Hymn

Once in royal David's city
Stood a lowly cattle shed,
Where a mother laid her Baby
In a manger for His bed:
Mary was that mother mild,
Jesus Christ her little Child.

He came down to earth from heaven,
Who is God and Lord of all,
And His shelter was a stable,
And His cradle was a stall;
With the poor, and mean, and lowly,
Lived on earth our Savior holy.

And through all His wondrous childhood
He would honor and obey,
Love and watch the lowly maiden,
In whose gentle arms He lay:
Christian children all must be
Mild, obedient, good as He.

And our eyes at last shall see Him,
Through His own redeeming love;
For that Child so dear and gentle
Is our Lord in heaven above,
And He leads His children on
To the place where He is gone.

The First Day:
Morning

The Christmas Curiosity of the Angels (1)

To them it was revealed that, not to themselves, but to us they were ministering the things which now have been reported to you through those who have preached the gospel to you by the Holy Spirit sent from heaven—things which angels desire to look into.
1 Peter 1:12

There has always been a tremendous interest in Christmas, and now there seems to be an equal interest in angels. Angels are on television and in magazines. Angel sales are sky-rocketing. Angel books continue to flood the market. Angel pins and angel figurines are constantly seen.

Polls indicate that most people believe in the existence of angels. One poll showed that forty-six percent of Americans believe they have a guardian angel.

The Bible is also interested in angels, so much so that its authors mention them 273 times (108 in the Old Testament, and 165 in the New).

While there is a constant and ongoing interest in angels, that interest increases each Christmas. The Christmas season inevitably makes us think of angels. The angel Gabriel was given the responsibility of announcing the forthcoming birth of John the Baptist, Christ's forerunner (Luke 1:11-20) to his father Zacharias, as well as the forthcoming birth of Jesus to His mother Mary (Luke 1:26-33).

A single angel announced the birth of Jesus to shepherds outside Bethlehem (Luke 2:8-12). No sooner were the words out of his mouth than he was joined by "a multitude of the heavenly host" who burst into praise of God (Luke 2:13-14).

It is evident, then, that angels were closely associated with Christmas.

The Angels Are Interested in Salvation

The association of angels with Christmas runs far deeper, however, than merely announcing it. In this text, the apostle Peter asserts that the angels are intensely curious about the very matter Christmas was designed to deal with, that is, the salvation of sinners.

Simon Peter could not get over this business of salvation. To him it was the most marvelous and glorious thing imaginable. After addressing his readers (vv.1-2), he immediately launches into a song of praise to God about salvation. He thanks God for the "abundant mercy" that has given believers "a living hope" (v.3). He rejoices in the "inheritance" that is "reserved in heaven" for believers (v.4). And he freely and gladly acknowledges that all of this is made possible in and through the Lord Jesus Christ (vv.3,7).

From this burst of praise for salvation, the apostle proceeded to make it clear to his readers that it fulfilled the prophecies of the Old Testament (vv.11-12). This was only one of many evidences that the work of Christ was genuine and could be completely trusted.

Specifically, Peter asserts that the prophets of the Old

Testament were enabled by "the Spirit of Christ" (v.11) to see both "the sufferings of Christ and the glories that would follow" (v.11).

Suddenly and unexpectedly Peter brings his discussion of this matter to a close by adding this phrase: "things which angels desire to look into" (v.12).

The Greek word translated "look into" is the same word used to describe what Peter himself did when he came to the tomb of the risen Christ. We are told that he stooped down and looked into the tomb (John 20:5). The same word is used of Mary Magdalene when she also looked into the tomb of Christ (John 20:11).

By using this word, Peter portrays the angels bending over, or, as it were, leaning over the balcony rail of heaven to carefully and intently peer down upon the earth so they can see what God has done and is doing in and through the Lord Jesus Christ.

The Old Testament depicts the very same thing. On top of the Ark of the Covenant was the mercy seat, where the blood of atonement was sprinkled by the high priest. And on each side of that mercy seat was a golden cherub looking down at the very spot where the blood was sprinkled (Ex. 25:18-22).

Cherubim were also depicted on the veil that separated the Most Holy Place from the Holy Place of the tabernacle (Ex. 26:31). The Most Holy Place was that chamber into which the high priest entered once a year to sprinkle the blood on the mercy seat. The depiction of the cherubim on that heavy veil also conveys the desire of the angels to look into salvation through the shedding of blood.

To Think About

- God's salvation plan for people is so significant that it captures the interest of angels! If angels marvel, and are amazed by the work of sending Jesus, how much more should ordinary humans be!

- There is a sense in which we are even more privileged than angels, for we receive a benefit from Christmas that angels can never receive. Jesus died for human beings, not for angels!

Evening

The Christmas Curiosity of the Angels (2)

To them it was revealed that, not to themselves, but to us they were ministering the things which now have been reported to you through those who have preached the gospel to you by the Holy Spirit sent from heaven — things which angels desire to look into.

1 Peter 1:12

Why Angels Are Interested. . .

Why are the angels so interested in the salvation of sinners? We are not surprised to read that the prophets of the Old Testament "inquired and searched carefully" (v.10) regarding this matter of salvation. We can well understand them desiring to understand better those truths which they were prophesying. But what is this about the angels? Why do they marvel at the mercy of God?

We are out of our element here. Perhaps they study salvation out of amazement that God could love those who had so grievously sinned against Him and were, therefore, deserving of nothing but His wrath. The book of Jude tells us that there were also angels who fell into sin. These "did not keep their proper domain" because they rebelled against God, but there was no salvation provided for them. They have rather been "reserved in everlasting chains under darkness for the judgment of the great day…" (Jude 6, see also 2 Peter 2:4). The fact there was no salvation offered for the fallen angels must have made salvation for fallen men and women even more amazing to the angels in heaven.

Perhaps the unfallen angels study salvation out of amazement that the Prince of Glory, the eternal Son of God, would stoop so low as to take to Himself the humanity of sinners, and in that humanity would suffer the hostility of sinners and die on a Roman cross.

Perhaps they study salvation out of amazement at the peace and joy of those who have received it. Could it be that there is among the angels a bit of envy (sinless envy, of course) for those of us who have been saved? Do the angels in heaven, who have not sinned and never needed mercy, find themselves wishing that they could experience the joy that such mercy brings? The author of this verse seemed to think along these lines:

> *When I sing redemption's story,*
> *The angels will fold their wings;*
> *For angels never knew the joy*
> *That my salvation brings.*

There is yet another reason the angels are so keenly interested in salvation. The angels are interested in anything that brings glory to God, and nothing so glorifies God as His wonderful work of salvation. This work displays His grace, His justice and His wisdom in such a way that the angels, who delight in His glory, cannot help but be fascinated by it.

In all likelihood the angels marvel at our salvation for all of these reasons and perhaps for reasons that have never even occurred to us.

The Challenge to Us

It is all well and good to know that the angels are interested in salvation, but what does it have to do with us? The fact is their interest in our redemption speaks a very powerful word to us.

The angels are God's mighty ones who "excel in strength" (Ps. 103:20). The angels are God's immortal ones who are beyond the reach of death. The angels are God's faithful ones who ceaselessly and perfectly serve the God who made them (Heb. 1:7). And they stand in awe of redemption.

If God's mighty, immortal and faithful ones stand in awe of redemption, how much more should those who are weak, dying, and sinful. If angels, who have never experienced salvation, are so keenly interested in it, how keen an interest should those have who have experienced it!

Is this the case? Is this characteristic of people who profess to know the Lord? Are we keenly interested in our Christ and the salvation He has provided? Is it evident to others that this is the main thing in our lives? Is there among us a keen interest in learning more about our salvation? Do we seize opportunities to study the Word of God? Do we have a keen interest in expressing gratitude to God for our salvation? Are we anxious to join in public worship and sing praises to His name? Are we eager to do whatever we can to advance His kingdom?

Can we take the following words and truthfully say them to ourselves:

Pause, my soul! adore and wonder!
Ask, "O why such love to me?"
Grace has put me in the number
Of the Savior's family;
Hallelujah!
Thanks, Eternal Love, to thee!

To Think About

▶ In New Testament times, some Christians began drifting away from the Lord and neglecting their salvation (see Heb. 2:1-4). What would the author say if he could observe us for a while? Would his assessment of us be the same as it was of those to whom he wrote? Would he accuse us of neglecting "so great a salvation"? (Heb. 2:3).

▶ It is such a great salvation that the angels of heaven themselves are intrigued by it. May God help us to see the greatness of it and to rejoice in it. Let's learn from the angels. Let's allow their interest in salvation to rebuke us for our lack of interest and to renew us in fervent desire to worship and to serve the Lord.

The Second Day:
Morning

God's Special Christmas Angel—Gabriel (1)

*Now while I was speaking, praying, and confessing my sin
and the sin of my people Israel, and presenting my supplica-
tion before the LORD my God for the holy mountain of my God,
yes, while I was speaking in prayer, the man Gabriel, whom I
had seen in the vision at the beginning, being caused to fly
swiftly, reached me about the time of the evening offering.*
Daniel 9:20, 21a
Read Daniel 9:20-27

Christmas has to do with the salvation of ordinary
people—sinners. Christ came to Bethlehem so He
could go to Calvary and there offer Himself as a substitute for those who would trust Him.

We have seen that the angels are keenly interested in
this matter of salvation. Since Christmas has to do with
salvation, it is legitimate to say angels are interested in
Christmas.

It is not enough, however, only to say that angels are
acutely interested in salvation. Their association with
Christmas goes much farther than that. Angels were also
deeply involved in announcing Christmas. An angel
appeared to Joseph to announce that Mary would bear a
Son who was to be named "Jesus" because He would
"save His people from their sins" (Matt. 1:21). An angel
appeared on the night Jesus was born to announce the

good news to shepherds (Luke 2:9).

No angel was more engaged in announcing the birth of Christ than Gabriel. The Bible records four appearances of Gabriel—two in Daniel and two in Luke—and three of these appearances were to do with Christmas.

The first of Gabriel's three Christmas appearances came almost five hundred years before Christmas became a reality. On this occasion he appeared to Daniel in Babylon (Dan. 9:20-27). Daniel had been reading the Scriptures to ascertain exactly when his people's period of captivity in Babylon would come to an end. Suddenly Gabriel appeared and announced that he had come to give him understanding (Dan. 9:2,22).

Daniel, of course, expected to be given understanding on the matter with which he was occupied, that is, the end of his people's captivity. But Gabriel came to give him insight into a far greater matter: the coming of Christ. In effect Gabriel was sent to Daniel to lift his eyes off the pressing issue of the present (the date of Israel's release from captivity) to an event of far greater importance.

Gabriel's second Christmas appearance was to Zacharias (Luke 1:5-20). On this occasion he announced the forthcoming birth of John the Baptist, the forerunner of Christ, to Zacharias.

Six months after appearing to Zacharias, Gabriel appeared to Mary to announce the forthcoming birth of the Savior (Luke 1:26-38).

The Christmas part of Gabriel's appearances might well lead us to refer to him as "God's Christmas angel." On the other hand, the "announcing" part of these occasions has led some to refer to him as "God's preaching angel."

The Purpose of Christ's Coming

As we examine the preaching of Gabriel on these occasions, we see certain major themes emerge. We may say Gabriel preached the purpose of announcing Christ's coming.

In his message to Daniel, Gabriel said the Messiah would be "cut off, but not for Himself" (Dan. 9:26), that is, He would die but His death would be for others. Through that death He would "finish the transgression", "make an end of sins", "make reconciliation for iniquity", "bring in everlasting righteousness", "seal up the vision and prophecy" (fulfill prophecy), and "anoint the Most Holy" (Dan. 9:24).

There could be no better statement of the redeeming work of Christ. He died not for himself but for others, and in doing so provided forgiveness for their sins and eternal righteousness before God. After dying on the cross, the Lord Jesus entered into heaven to make intercession for His people and thus anointed "the Most Holy". All of this not only fulfilled the prophecies of Daniel but many other prophecies of the Old Testament as well.

To Think About

- God communicates! Angels are, literally, messengers, ones whose responsibilities include taking messages from God to people. In the purposes of God, centuries before Jesus came to this world, God was beginning to prepare people for the wonderful news of the Savior who was to come!

- What an encouragement to consider the Old Testament's prophetic message of the coming of Jesus. How much more may we enjoy the clarity of the New Testament revelation of Jesus!

God's Special Christmas Angel—Gabriel (2)

*Then Mary said to the angel, "How can this be, since I do not
know a man?" And the angel answered and said to her,
"The Holy Spirit will come upon you, and the power of the
Highest will overshadow you; therefore, also, that Holy One
who is to be born will be called the Son of God.*
Luke 1:34,35
See also Luke 1:5-20, 26-38

The Manner of Christ's Coming

When he came to Mary, Gabriel stressed the manner
of Christ's coming. Christ was to be born like no
other. He was to be born of a virgin.

Gabriel explained it to Mary in these words: "The Holy
Spirit will come upon you, and the power of the Highest
will overshadow you; therefore, also, that Holy One who
is to be born will be called the Son of God" (Luke 1:35).

The virgin birth has been much disputed in recent
years, but the evidence for it is inescapable. Two of the
Gospel writers, Matthew and Luke, deal with it. Luke's
account of the virgin birth is especially noteworthy because he was a physician and would have been naturally
skeptical of the possibility of a virgin birth. He begins his
Gospel by telling us that he had examined carefully the
entire gospel story. His words "having perfect understanding of all things from the very first" (Luke 1:3)

amount to him saying he had "traced all things accurately." In other words, Luke's Gospel is the product of the painstaking research of a man not given to readily accepting myths and superstitions; and yet he gives the fullest account of the virgin birth!

Gabriel's message on the virgin birth emphasized an essential part of the gospel message. There could be no salvation for sinners without it. It is that important! The Second Person of the Trinity had to take our humanity in order to save us, but He also had to be different from us. If He had not been born of a virgin, He would have been exactly like us and could not, therefore, have done anything for us. In other words, He would have been a sinner himself and in need of redemption.

An Everlasting Kingdom

In his appearance to Mary, Gabriel also stressed the duration of Christ's kingdom: "And He will reign over the house of Jacob forever, and of His kingdom there will be no end" (Luke 1: 33).

Centuries before God made this promise to King David of Israel: "I will set up your seed after you, who will come from your body, and I will establish His kingdom forever…. And your house and your kingdom shall be established forever before you. Your throne shall be established forever" (2 Sam. 7:12b,16).

That promise was now to be fulfilled. Jesus Christ is the king who reigns forever, not over an earthly, political kingdom, but rather over a spiritual kingdom. This rule, now in the hearts of His people, will culminate in a kingdom of glory that will be universally acknowledged (Luke 17:21; John 18:36-37; Rom. 14:17; Phil. 2:9-11).

What a joy it is to be part of such a kingdom! When other kings and kingdoms have crumbled and passed away, the kingdom of our Lord shall endure!

The importance of having true faith

Gabriel appeared to Zacharias to announce that he and his wife would soon become the parents of a very special son, John the Baptist. He would play a unique role in God's plan by preparing the way for the Messiah (Luke 1:17). The birth of this special son meant the long-awaited Messiah was, as it were, standing right at the door!

But Zacharias and his wife were well advanced in years. They could not have a child! (Luke 1:18). The thing was impossible! So Zacharias gave way to unbelief, and, as a result, was stricken with a severe judgment, namely, being unable to speak until after John the Baptist was born (Luke 1:20, 23,63-64).

While Zacharias refused to believe Gabriel's message, Mary quickly and readily embraced his message to her although she had an even greater obstacle to her faith. Zacharias knew that something like this had happened in the past—Abraham and Sarah had also been asked to believe that God would give them a son in their old age (Gen. 18:1-15). There was, however, no precedent for Mary. No virgin had ever conceived and borne a son.

To Think About

- Be thankful that the virgin birth is a fact of history, that Mary had an attitude of obedience and faith, making herself available to doing the will of God!

- Zacharias reminds us that it is possible to be an unbelieving believer, that is, to actually be a child of God and still refuse to believe the Word of God at one point or another. It is always tragic to see someone who believes in God and His Word fail to believe at a given point. It is much sadder to see someone never come to faith in God at all. The unbelieving believer robs himself of God's blessings, while the unbeliever robs himself of eternity in heaven with God.

- How we need to take all of this to heart! So far as we know Gabriel is not these days appearing to individuals to preach the glorious gospel of Jesus Christ. But that message is still being preached. And with the preaching of it is the call to believe.

Morning

The Christmas Joy of the Angels (1)

And suddenly there was with the angel a multitude of the
heavenly host praising God and saying:
"Glory to God in the highest,
And on earth peace, goodwill toward men!
Luke 2:13,14
Read Luke 2:8-14

We know the angels are capable of joy. The book of Job tells us they shouted for joy as they watched God perform His work of creation (Job 38:7).

The joy of the angels on that occasion must have been very great indeed. How amazing to hear God speak a mere word and then see something pop into existence! Perhaps the angels exclaimed, "Oh!" and "Ah!" as they witnessed one act of creation after another. Perhaps we do not go too far astray if we imagine them conversing as they watched. A particular act of creation may very well have caused one to say: "Wow! That was a good one!" Another act may have caused yet another angel to say: "That's the one I like!"

How did the angels respond when they saw the first man, Adam, spring forth as a result of God stooping down, taking a handful of dust and breathing into it? (Gen. 2:7). There must have been some "Ohs" and "Ahs" then. This man, a little lower than the angels themselves

(Heb. 2:7), was God's special creature. He was made in the image of God (Gen. 1:26), crowned with glory and honor, and set over all the works of God's hands (Heb. 2:7).

And what of the angels when man, that special creature of honor and glory, suddenly turned upon his Creator and sinned so grievously against Him (Gen. 3:1–7)? Is it safe to say their joy turned to sorrow?

After Adam and Eve's sin, the Lord stationed cherubim at the entrance of the Garden of Eden. They, with their flaming sword, were to "guard the way to the tree of life" (Gen. 3:24).

Did those mighty heavenly beings look with sorrow and wonderment first at the tree of life there in the garden and then at Adam and Eve sadly walking away?

So what was there about God creating that would cause the angels to rejoice? What was there about man's rebellion that caused them to grieve?

We know the angels are utterly devoted to God and to His glory. They find inexpressible joy in anything that brings glory to God, and sorrow in anything that robs God of His glory. They rejoiced over God's creative work because it brought glory to God. It put His wisdom, His omnipotence, His sovereignty, and His grace on display.

Conversely, they sorrowed over man's sin because the very essence of sin is falling short of the glory of God (Rom. 3:23). It is the creature thumbing his nose in the face of the Creator and saying: "I will not have you ruling over me. I will be God myself."

Evidence of Angelic Joy

If the angels of God so rejoiced over His creative work and so sorrowed over that creative work being marred by sin, we should not be surprised to learn that they rejoiced at the birth of Christ.

In fact we may go so far as to say their joy on that occasion far surpassed that which they experienced at creation. The greatness of their joy the night Jesus was born is abundantly evident. It is there in the words of the single angel, the herald, who announced the birth to the shepherds: "Do not be afraid, for behold, I bring you good tidings of great joy which will be to all people" (v.10).

It is there in the anthem from the heavenly host that suddenly appeared to those shepherds: "Glory to God in the highest, And on earth peace, goodwill toward men!" (v.14).

The phrase "heavenly host" seems to suggest a great number of angels were present. How many angels are there? The psalmist says:

The chariots of God are twentythousand,
Even thousands of thousands; ...

(Ps. 68:17).

In the book of Revelation, the apostle John says he saw "ten thousand times ten thousand and thousands of thousands" angels around the throne of God (Rev. 5:11).

We do not know how many of those angels joined in the anthem that the shepherds heard, but we may be sure it was an impressive number indeed. The phrase "heavenly host" may also suggest every kind of angel was present. It would not be surprising if the heavenly host in the skies above Bethlehem consisted of some of each category of angels.

To Think About

▶ The angels of heaven rejoice when God is glorified. Nothing has ever brought more glory to God than this matter of Christmas. Nothing has so glorified Him as His Son taking to Himself our humanity and, in that humanity, providing redemption for us.

▶ There are several ways in which the Lord Jesus Christ, who was going to redeem sinners, was going to bring glory to God. See if you can think of one or two. The next reading will suggest several reasons.

The Third Day:
Evening

The Christmas Joy of the Angels (2)

*Then the angel said to them, "Do not be afraid, for behold, I
bring you good tidings of great joy which will be to all people. For there is born to you this day in the city of David a
Savior, who is Christ the Lord."*
Luke 2:10,11

Reasons for Angelic Joy

It is not enough to merely observe the joy the angels
experienced when Jesus was born. We must ask why
they felt this joy. What was there about the birth of Jesus
that made this such a joyous event for the very angels of
heaven?

The grace of God
The redeeming work of Christ glorified the grace of God.
God would have been perfectly just if He had done
nothing at all to redeem guilty sinners. He could have
merely left all of us to the results of our sin, and no one
could have accused Him of being unfair.

But He was unwilling to do so. Instead He made a way
for us to be forgiven of our sins and to be restored to
fellowship with Himself. That way was and is His Son,
Jesus Christ. It was grace that compelled the Father to
give the Son, and it was grace that compelled the Son to
leave heaven and come to this dark world.

The justice of God

By His redeeming work, the Lord Jesus also magnified or glorified the justice of God. It was not enough for the Son of God to come to this world. He could not have saved us by merely coming *to* this world. He had to do something specific while *in* this world. He had to satisfy the justice of God.

How few people today realize this! God's justice had to be satisfied in order for us to be saved! There could never be salvation apart from this! From the very beginning, God decreed death as the penalty for sin, not just physical death, but also spiritual and eternal death.

That penalty had to be paid! If God had just set it aside, He would have not been true to His own word. God himself could not have let a single sinner go free without that penalty being paid. Here is the gloriously good news of the gospel: on the cross the Lord Jesus paid that penalty for guilty sinners. Yes, the Lord Jesus actually endured on that cross an eternity's worth of separation from God on behalf of sinners. There He cried out: "My God, My God, why have You forsaken Me?" (Matt. 27:46).

God was just to demand that the penalty for sin be paid once, but He would have been unjust to demand payment twice. If, therefore, Jesus paid the penalty for me, there is no penalty left for me to pay! Yes, by His death on the cross, the Lord Jesus magnified the justice of God.

The wisdom of God

Furthermore, we can say that the Lord Jesus Christ also magnified the wisdom of God. We might say the cross of

Christ solved a tremendous difficulty, namely, how God could at one and the same time judge sin and let the sinner go free. Or we can put it in this way: how could God both satisfy His grace and His justice?

His grace demanded that a way be found to forgive sinners. His justice demanded that sinners be punished eternally. God, in His infinite wisdom, made a way. Through the death of His Son on the cross, God satisfied both the demands of His grace and His justice. Justice saw the Lord Jesus Christ suffering in the place of sinners, and was satisfied. Because Jesus took the penalty for believing sinners, there is no penalty left for them to pay and grace also is satisfied.

To Think About

▶ The redemptive work of Christ put the grace, the justice, the wisdom of God and much more on display, and thus brought glory to God. And the angels, who rejoice when God is glorified, rejoiced in this work. They rejoiced when Jesus was born because that was the beginning of the work He had come to do.

▶ Bethlehem was going to lead to Calvary. The birth of Jesus was a preparation for His death. How fitting it was for the angels to rejoice above the fields of Bethlehem!

▶ When the shepherds heard the good news, they rejoiced! They went to Bethlehem, saw the child and returned to their flocks "glorifying and praising God for all the things that they had heard and seen" (Luke 2:20). We can follow their example. We can and must rejoice because the Savior over whom the angels and shepherds rejoiced still lives and still saves. Now that is cause for true joy!

The Fourth Day:

Morning

The Christmas Sorrow of the Angels (1)

For to which of the angels did He ever say:
"You are My Son, Today I have begotten You"?
And again:
"I will be to Him a Father,
And He shall be to Me a Son"?
But when He again brings the firstborn into the world, He says:
"Let all the angels of God worship Him."
Hebrews 1:5-6

The angels of heaven rejoiced over the birth of the Lord Jesus Christ because it marked the beginning of His redeeming work in history, a work that was designed to bring glory to God. The angels always rejoice when God is glorified.

If it is legitimate to speak of the Christmas joy of angels, it would also seem to be legitimate to speak of the Christmas sorrow of angels. But what is there about Christmas that would cause the angels to be sorrowful? The author of the book of Hebrews provides insight on this matter. He writes to Jews who had made a profession of faith in Christ but had begun to waver. Some of them had begun to wonder if they had been right to forsake Judaism and profess Christ.

So this author takes up his pen and begins to write. He devotes more than half of his letter to demonstrating for his readers the superiority of Christ. He does this by showing how those persons and things most venerated by Judaism pale in comparison to Christ. Moses, the priesthood, and the temple itself cannot begin to compare with the Lord Jesus.

The angels were among those most venerated by the Jews, so much so that the author begins his presentation of the superiority of Christ by showing how He far surpasses the very angels themselves.

The author drives this point home by making note of what God has not said to the angels (v.5) and then what He has said to them (v.6).

What God Has Not Said to the Angels
What is it that God has not said to the angels? The author takes his readers to Psalm 2:7 for words that God the Father spoke to His Son:

You are My Son, Today I have begotten You.

The Second Person of the Trinity is and has always been the eternal Son of God. The Bible commentator John Gill correctly observes: "Christ is the Son of God, not by creation, nor by adoption, nor by office, but by nature; He is the true, proper, natural, and eternal Son of God."

The above verse cannot mean then that Jesus became the Son at the incarnation. Rather, it refers to the Father declaring Him to be what He had in fact always been: the Son. The Father made such a declaration at Jesus' baptism (Matt. 3:17) and on the Mount of Transfiguration (Matt. 17:5). But the Father issued His supreme declaration of Christ's Sonship by raising Him from the dead (Acts 13:33; Rom. 1:4).

God the Father has never made such a declaration to an angel. It is true that angels are referred to as sons of God in the book of Job (Job 38:7), but this is in a collective sense. God has never said to any single angel: "You are My Son." But He has said that to Jesus Christ, and the fact He has said it shows the superiority of Christ.

Having established this, the author takes his readers to 2 Samuel 7:14 for additional words God has spoken to the Son:

I will be to Him a Father, And He shall be to Me a Son.

These words, originally spoken to David, looked beyond David's immediate son, Solomon, to a far greater descendant, the Lord Jesus Christ. While Jesus was a physical descendant of David, He was much more than that. He was also God in human flesh, the Son of God.

What God Has Said to the Angels
The author of Hebrews shows his readers what God has said to the angels by drawing some text from Psalm 97:7: *Let all the angels of God worship Him* (v. 6).

The author says God spoke these words to the angels "when He again brings the firstborn into the world". The word "again" has caused some to think of the second coming of Christ. That would seem to be the time when God "again" brings Jesus into this world.

Since the previous verses deal with the incarnation and since the angels obviously worshipped Jesus at that time (Luke 2:14), it is probably correct to translate the phrase: "And again, when He brings the firstborn into the world, ..."

In other words, the author is not using the word "again" to refer to Christ coming again, but rather to an additional argument for the point he is making—that is, the superiority of Christ over the angels.

His point is quite plain. Some of his readers were thinking about forsaking Christ and going back to Judaism, a system which venerated the angels. But if the readers went back, they would be making a colossal mistake in doing so because the angels themselves worship Jesus!

To Think About

▶ Consider what a privilege it is for us to have received the knowledge of the Son of God born as a baby; what could be greater news than to know that God was stepping directly into our world and was about to demonstrate His power in providing redemption!

▶ Angels are insistent that they themselves should receive no such thing as worship or veneration. Suggest several reasons why people today might be interested in worshiping angels. What would you say to such a person? What can you do to avoid falling into the trap of angel worship?

The Christmas Sorrow of the Angels (2)

Let no one cheat you of your reward, taking delight in false
humility and worship of angels, intruding into those things
which he has not seen, vainly puffed up by his fleshly mind.
Colossians 2:18

Things That Cause the Angels to Sorrow

The angels worshipped Jesus the night He came to this world, they worship Him now, and they will worship Him with the redeemed (Rev. 5: 11-12). And they are saddened when He is not given the worship He deserves.

This morning's reading made the point that angels, privileged beings, received veneration, but they themselves were far more intent on beholding the glories of the Christ who was to come into this world. Imagine the sorrow such beings might feel when humans think that worship should be given to any being other than the Lord Jesus Christ.

And yet, this is, in fact, what happens quite often. Worship that should be directed to Christ is being directed to others. The angels themselves are, shockingly, being made objects of worship.

The Bible plainly forbids this. The angels are servants of God (Heb. 1:7), and God alone is to be worshipped. The apostle Paul writes to the Christians in Colossae:

"Let no one cheat you of your reward, taking delight in false humility and worship of angels, intruding into those things which he has not seen, vainly puffed up by his fleshly mind" (Col. 2:18).

Furthermore, the apostle John, as he penned the book of Revelation, twice received from angels the stern command that he was not to worship them. John describes the first incident in this way: "And I fell at his feet to worship him. But he said to me, 'See that you do not do that! I am your fellow servant, and of your brethren who have the testimony of Jesus. Worship God! For the testimony of Jesus is the spirit of prophecy'" (Rev. 19:10).

The second incident is described in similar words: "Now I, John, saw and heard these things. And when I heard and saw, I fell down to worship before the feet of the angel who showed me these things. Then he said to me, 'See that you do not do that. For I am your fellow servant, and of your brethren the prophets, and of those who keep the words of this book. Worship God'" (Rev. 22:8-9).

In this age of angel-mania, we urgently need to remember John's experiences. Angels are not to be worshipped. God is. Angels are not to be offered prayer. God is. Angels are not to be praised. God is. Angels are not to be served. God is. The very angels this age so reveres are happiest when we are worshipping God, praying to God, praising God and serving God.

Why would anyone worship angels instead of the God who made the angels? An article in *Time* Magazine offered this explanation: "For those who choke too easily on God and His rules ... angels are the handy compromise, all fluff and meringue, kind, non-judgmental. They are available to everyone like aspirin."

A *Christianity Today* article once said: "Angels too easily provide a temptation for those who want a 'fix' of spirituality without bothering with God Himself."

We may prefer angels to God, but God has never allowed us to worship according to our personal preferences. Since He is the only proper object or focus of worship, it must be done the way He wants it done.

Furthermore, there is no salvation in angels. No angel has offered himself as a substitute for sinners, but Jesus Christ did. He alone is the Savior. To run around Christ—who holds in His hands the gift of salvation—and to worship angels instead is akin to running around someone who holds a diamond in his hand in order to receive from someone else a worthless stone.

We are not completely out of danger if we merely refuse to worship angels. We must be very careful that we give no one the worship and honor that belong to Christ. There has been in the last several years an alarming tendency among ordinary Bible-believing Christians to bestow adulation upon Mary.

The Lord Jesus Himself addressed this matter. He was speaking on a certain occasion when a woman from His audience suddenly cried out: "Blessed is the womb that bore You, and the breasts which nursed You!" (Luke 11:27).

The woman was, of course, quite right. Mary had indeed received a special blessing from the Lord. But her blessing did not mean that she was to be placed on a level with the Lord or to receive worship. The Lord Jesus pointed this woman to the true priority by saying:

"More than that blessed are those who hear the word of God and keep it!" (Luke 11:28).

The word of God to which Jesus directed her attention was very plain on this matter of worship. It is God and God alone who is to be worshipped (Deut. 6:13; 10:20; Matt. 4:10).

All the angels of heaven understand that the triune God is to be worshipped. Mary herself understood that the Son she bore was to be the object of her worship (Acts 1:14). We most honor all the angels and Mary when we worship their God. We must worship God and Him alone with all our heart, soul, mind and strength.

To Think About

- We are blessed when we hear the word of God and do the will of God—even more blessed than the Mary the mother of Jesus. See Luke 11:27-28. You can be sure to pay attention to the will of God by reading His Word, the Bible.

- What kind of things might cause people to turn back from following Christ in the days in which we live? How can a consideration of the birth of Jesus, the God-man, help them to get back on track in their worship of Him who is the true and living God?

The Fifth Day:

Morning

Christmas for the Fearful (1)

Now it came to pass in the days of Ahaz the son of Jotham, the son of Uzziah, king of Judah, that Rezin king of Syria and Pekah the son of Remaliah, king of Israel, went up to Jerusalem to make war against it, but could not prevail against it. And it was told to the house of David, saying, "Syria's forces are deployed in Ephraim." So his heart and the heart of his people were moved as the trees of the woods are moved with the wind.
Isaiah 7:1,2

Most of us are familiar with the "Ful" family. We spend a good bit of our time with them. Some of them are very appealing. Joyful, Prayerful, Hopeful and Faithful are among the most attractive.

Other members of this family are unsavory characters to say the least. There are, to name just a few, Fearful, Sorrowful, Doubtful, and Sinful.

Sadly enough, many of us spend more time with the repulsive members of the family than we do with the attractive members! They always seem to be knocking at the door, and, all too often, we let them in. And they are guests that never want to go home! Well, I have good news for all those who have been hosting the unsavory "Fuls." Among all the many benefits and blessings of Christmas, we can and must acknowledge this: Christmas deals in a marvelous way with the dreadful members of the "Ful" family. It has the capacity to drive them from us and to bring peace and tranquility in their stead.

The prophecy of Isaiah brings before us the sad spectacle of a man who was entertaining one of the "Ful" family. Here we have Ahaz, king of Judah, entertaining none other than that nasty and despicable character, Mr. Fearful. Verse two of the passage before us says of Ahaz: "So his heart and the heart of his people were moved as the trees of the woods are moved with the wind."

In other words, Ahaz and his people were frightened, terribly frightened. They were so afraid that their hearts were trembling within them.

The Fear of Ahaz and Judah

What was the source of their fear? One of their neighbors, Assyria, was rapidly gaining strength as the major world power of the day. Kings of smaller nations viewed her expansion with great alarm and began forming alliances with each other. Pekah, king of Israel, and Rezin, king of Syria, had formed an alliance with each other, and they were pressuring Ahaz to join them.

Ahaz thought he knew a better way to stave off the Assyrian threat and thus secure the future of his kingdom. He decided to make an alliance with Assyria herself. That decision angered the kings of Israel and Syria so much that they decided to go to war against Judah.

As this chapter opens, Ahaz receives the word of the advancing forces of Syria, and he is filled with a sense of dread and foreboding. What would happen to him and his people? How could they possibly hope to survive this threat?

Isaiah's Cheering Message: A Gracious Promise

While these and other questions churned and pounded in Ahaz's fevered brain, the Lord sent the prophet Isaiah to him with this cheering message of hope: "Take heed, and be quiet; do not fear or be fainthearted for these two stubs of smoking firebrands, for the fierce anger of Rezin and Syria, and the son of Remaliah. . . . thus says the Lord GOD: 'It shall not stand, nor shall it come to pass'" (vv.4,7).

In other words, the Lord was telling Ahaz not to fear the kings of Israel and Syria and their armies. No matter what these enemies were plotting to do against Judah, the Lord had determined that their plans would not stand. Man's plans never stand when the Lord decides they should fall!

To Think About

- Our circumstances may be bleaker than they have ever been before; we may be plagued by fear—and yet there is a word of comfort to us in our fear if we will just listen to what God will say to us, on His terms, in His Word, the Bible.

- Fear may lead a person to seek solutions from the wrong sources. Think of two or three areas in your life where you think you might be tempted to try to find a solution to a problem that does not take into consideration the revealed will of God.

The Fifth Day:
Evening

Christmas for the Fearful (2)

Therefore the Lord Himself will give you a sign: Behold, the virgin shall conceive and bear a Son, and shall call His name Immanuel.
Isaiah 7:14
Read Isaiah 7:1-14

Isaiah's Cheering Message: A Gracious Sign

God gave Ahaz a gracious word, as we saw in this morning's reading. After this, the Lord proceeded to urge him to ask for a sign (v.11). How the grace of God shines and sparkles in this account! The fact the Lord ever speaks at all is sheer grace. The fact that the Lord gave Ahaz, a wicked king, the opportunity to ask for a sign is staggeringly gracious!

The Lord doesn't always express His grace in the same way, but He is always gracious. He is gracious to all in many ways, and He is gracious to His own in every way.

Ahaz responded to God's grace by stubbornly refusing to ask a sign. He knew if he asked for it, the Lord would give it, and he knew if the Lord gave it, he would be obligated to heed God's Word. He had no place in his life for that.

But God was not to be put off. Ahaz was going to have a sign whether he wanted one or not. The sign was that a virgin would bear a son and before that child was old

~ 48 ~

enough to know right from wrong, the threat posed by Israel and Syria would be completely eliminated.

A woman who was a virgin at the time Isaiah gave this prophecy would, through the process of natural generation, bear a son and name Him "Immanuel" ("God with us") and both Syria and Israel would be destroyed early in the life of this child. We may quibble over the exact identity of this child (perhaps it was Isaiah's son), but this much is clear: Syria and Israel were both destroyed just as Isaiah prophesied, the former in 732 B.C. and the latter in 722 B.C.).

The greater fulfillment of Isaiah's prophecy came with the birth of the Lord Jesus. The first fulfillment required only that a young woman during Ahaz's time become pregnant and bear a son in the natural way. But Jesus Christ was truly virgin conceived and virgin born.

And while the child born during Ahaz's time signaled the presence of God with His people, the Lord Jesus Christ is in the fullest sense "Immanuel." He was nothing less than God in human flesh. Therefore, all during His earthly life, God was with people in a special way.

We might say then that God's way of treating Ahaz's fear was by pointing him beyond the dilemma that was vexing him to the glorious truth of Christmas. God treated his fear by calling him to look beyond his present circumstances to the coming Christ! It's almost as if the prophet said: "Ahaz, the final cure for fear does not rest in the defeat of Israel and Syria but in the coming of God's Son. This has been the hope of our people since our father Abraham, and you must make it your hope."

Our Fears

All kinds of fears haunt us: sickness, death, economic collapse, crime, environmental disaster, and war.

On the other hand, multitudes are utterly oblivious to the one thing they should fear: an eternity without God. The Lord Jesus pointed to this somber possibility in these words: "But I will show you whom you should fear: Fear Him who, after He has killed, has power to cast into hell; yes, I say to you, fear Him!" (Luke 12:5).

Thank God, there is good news for all who find themselves in the clutches of fear. That good news is contained in the ancient words of Isaiah to Ahaz: "Behold the virgin shall conceive and bear a Son, and shall call His name Immanuel."

We live on the other side of Christmas. Ahaz could only look forward to the fulfillment of these words. We can look back to Bethlehem's stable and see the fulfillment. There that night Immanuel was born. God took our humanity and took up residence among us, and, in doing so, knocked a gaping hole in fear. Child of God, what is your fear today? Bring it to Bethlehem and to the Immanuel born there. No matter how great it is, there is relief in that name "Immanuel." God is with us! He is with us to sympathize with us. He is with us to help us. He is with us to guide and instruct us. We can face anything that fear dishes out if we know we have the eternal God with us.

But can we say Immanuel is truly with us? The Bible says He died, rose again and ascended to the Father in heaven. How can He then be with His people? Jesus answered this question in these words: " … the Spirit of truth, whom the world cannot receive, because it neither sees Him nor knows Him; but you know Him, for He dwells with you and will be in you" (John 14:17).

There it is! Immanuel is still with His people through the ministry of the Holy Spirit whom He sent into the world.

Now I want to close this devotion and write a few words to readers who do not know Jesus Christ as Lord and Savior. I have already indicated that there is indeed something for you to fear, namely, eternity without God. I am happy to be able to say that you need fear this only if you reject the Lord Jesus Christ as your Lord and Savior. Call upon Him in repentance and faith today, and experience the blessing of His salvation!

To Think About

- Why did the Lord Jesus leave the glories of heaven to come to this world? Why did He take our humanity unto himself? Why did He become Immanuel? It was all for the purpose of providing salvation from sin and eternal destruction.

- That salvation has indeed been provided, and now the good news goes out that this salvation can and will be ours if we will break with our sins and trust completely in the atoning death of Jesus Christ. Those who trust Christ for salvation have nothing to fear when they stand before God. Instead they can join the apostle Paul in these triumphant words: "There is therefore now no condemnation to those who are in Christ Jesus…" (Rom. 8:1).

The Sixth Day:
Morning

Christmas for the Doubtful (1)

There shall come forth a Rod from the stem of Jesse,
And a Branch shall grow out of his roots.
The Spirit of the LORD shall rest upon Him,
The Spirit of wisdom and understanding,
The Spirit of counsel and might,
The Spirit of knowledge and of the fear of the LORD.
Isaiah 11:1-2

The prophet is here referring to the house of Jesse. It was a grand house indeed. It was from that house that great king David had sprung. Jesse was his father.

It was while David was king that God made some staggeringly glorious promises regarding the house of Jesse. David was told that the promised Messiah would come from among His descendants, and that the Messiah would be a king like no other. While all other kings rule for a limited period of time, the Messiah would reign forever (2 Sam. 7:16).

It would seem, in light of these promises, that the house of Jesse was destined to go from victory to victory without so much as a single lull. It would seem that the luster of the house of Jesse would never diminish.

The Miserable Condition of the House of Jesse
Now we fast forward several years to the time of Isaiah,

and the future house of Jesse is not so bright. It was a terribly serious time. The powerful Assyrian Empire was running around consuming her neighbors, and the nations that had not been overrun were nervous and afraid. Among these nervous nations was Judah. As her citizens surveyed the future, they found themselves wondering how long they could survive.

The survival of the nation was much more than a personal and political question. Bound up in it was this perplexing question: if the nation did not survive, what would become of all the glorious promises God had made to the house of Jesse? Specifically, what would become of that greatest of all the promises, the promise of the Messiah? The situation in Judah was so bleak at the time Isaiah was ministering that it appeared as if there would not even be a house of Jesse from which the Messiah could come. I can imagine several of the people of that time saying something like this: "Before the Messiah can get here the house of Jesse is going to be nothing more than a rotten stump."

In light of these things, we can say many in Judah were entertaining one of the more distasteful members of the "Ful" family—doubtful.

Fueled by the Assyrian crisis, their doubtfulness was destined to become even more pronounced in the future. The Assyrian crisis was to pass, but a far more serious crisis would take its place, one that would see the Babylonians come into the land of Judah, destroy the city of Jerusalem and the temple, and deport the king and most of the citizens.

Those who had to endure the Babylonian ordeal would have even more reason to shake their heads in dismay over the house of Jesse. At that time it would look as if Jesse's house was nothing but a dead, decaying stump.

The Message of the Prophet

Into this fog of doubt and uncertainty strode the prophet Isaiah with a clear and cheering message. First, the prophet assured his people that the Assyrian threat would be only temporary (10:24-25). Secondly, he declared that the Assyrian threat could not possibly make God forego or alter His promise to send the Messiah, nor, for that matter, could any other threat. God's promise was secure no matter how shaky it appeared to be.

The prophet firmly and triumphantly struck this note with these words: "There shall come forth a Rod from the stem of Jesse, and a Branch shall grow out of his roots" (v. 1).

The words "Rod" and "Branch," according to one Bible commentator, refer to a twig or shoot "such as starts up from the roots of a decayed tree."

The decayed tree was, of course, a reference to the house of Jesse. It looked as if it could not possibly survive, but as the prophet looked down the corridor of time, he was able to say to his countrymen: "Don't worry about that dead, decaying stump. From one of its decaying roots there will spring a twig."

That twig was, of course, none other than the Messiah Himself, the Lord Jesus Christ.

To Think About

- For people who do not believe the gospel, it seems easy to point fingers at circumstances and situations and to deny that God is working out history. But, seen through the lens of faith, what a different picture comes into focus!

- The fact is we live in an age of skepticism and doubt. Much of the Christian message is openly ridiculed. Christians try to stand firm against the doubt and skepticism of this day, but many find, before they know it, that Mr. Doubtful has made his way into their house and pulled up his chair to their table. They want to have faith, but they seem to find themselves frequently entertaining doubt.

- Doubt can obstruct faith. And yet, God will always have the last word. Think of several ways in which you, or your family and friends, might be inclined to doubt the certainty of God's work; and then consider how the narrative of both the Old and New Testaments shows the outworking of His purposes as He intends all things for good for those who love Him.

The Sixth Day:
Evening

Christmas for the Doubtful (2)

Now when He was asked by the Pharisees when the kingdom of God would come, He answered them and said, "The kingdom of God does not come with observation; nor will they say, 'See here!' or 'See there!' For indeed, the kingdom of God is within you."
Luke 17:20, 21

The Fulfillment of Isaiah's Prophecy

Let's fast forward again, this time to the opening of Matthew's Gospel. The first thing Matthew does is take us through a genealogy. In the midst of this genealogy, he tells us "Jesse begot David the king" (Matt. 1:6).

We knew that. But what about Jesse's house? Did it survive the terrible Assyrian crisis and the Babylonian Captivity? The Jews of those times probably expected future genealogists to record: "and the house of Jesse came to an end."

But as we read further in Matthew's genealogy we find no such statement. What we do find is this: "And Jacob begot Joseph the husband of Mary, of whom was born Jesus who is called Christ" (Matt. 1:16).

What looked to be a dead, dried up stump in Isaiah's day was not so dead after all. From the decayed stump of Jesse's house, the Lord Jesus Christ sprang up just as Isaiah had prophesied.

Matthew gives us the genealogy of Joseph because Joseph, while not Jesus' biological father, was His legal father. Legally, then, Jesus descended from the house of David. But He also physically descended from it because His mother, Mary, was also from the house of David.

Luke's Gospel records for us the visit of the angel Gabriel to deliver this message to Mary: "Do not be afraid, Mary, for you have found favor with God. And behold, you will conceive in your womb and bring forth a Son, and shall call His name JESUS. He will be great, and will be called the Son of the Highest; and the Lord God will give him the throne of His father David, And He will reign over the house of Jacob forever, and of His kingdom there will be no end" (Luke 1:30-33).

Jesus, a physical descendant of David, was born to Mary, just as God had promised to David in 2 Samuel 7, and just as He promised to the people of Judah through Isaiah the prophet. The stump was not dead after all.

Perhaps someone will suggest that one part of the original prophecy to David has failed. That prophecy required not only that the Christ spring from David's line but also that He reign forever, and Jesus, according to some, did not reign. This is true if we take His kingdom to be a temporal, political kingdom of this world. But the Lord Jesus himself insisted that His kingdom is not of this world (John 18:36), that it is in the hearts of His people (Luke 17:21).

The Lord Jesus Christ came to rule in and over His people, and there has never been a time in which that rule has not been in effect and there never will be a time when it will cease. To the contrary, Scripture assures us that this inward reign is destined not only to become open but also to be universally acknowledged. The apostle Paul says a day is coming in which every knee will bow before him and every tongue will confess that He is Lord (Phil. 2:9-11).

Isaiah himself was enabled to see that day, and he rejoiced in saying: "For the earth shall be full of knowledge of the LORD as the waters cover the sea" (Isa. 11:9).

The Glory of It All

Why is it important for us to take note of the promises that were originally given to Jesse's house and the subsequent decline that made it look as if those promises could never be fulfilled? Why is it important for us to note that those promises were fulfilled and are still being fulfilled?

The answer should be obvious. God has made promises to us as well. Our God is a promising God even to the point that His Word is fairly brimming with them.

One of the things that God has promised is that the same Lord Jesus who came to Bethlehem centuries ago is coming again. And when He comes He will take His people home to himself into realms of eternal glory where there will be no more sorrow, no more crying, no more pain, and no more death.

There are many "Assyrians" today who make it seem as if the promise of eternal glory cannot be fulfilled. Who are these Assyrians? They are all those people, beliefs, lifestyles, and circumstances that make the Word of God seem implausible and impossible.

What are Christians to do when Mr. Doubtful makes his way into their house and pulls up his chair to their table? The answer is this—we are to look into the Word of God for those many instances in which God fulfilled His promises even when it seemed impossible for Him to do so.

To Think About

- We do well to deduce from instances such as these that our God can be trusted. It does not matter, then, how weak the cause of God appears to be in these days. It doesn't matter how many modern "Assyrians" there are to assure us that the promises of God are false. Our hope does not lie in how things appear but rather in our faithful God.

- Each time Christmas rolls around, it has a way of correcting our course and of driving these kinds of doubts from us and bringing us back to where we ought to be. God fulfilled His promise to the house of Jesse, and He will fulfill His promises to us as well. Christmas reminds us not to look at dead stumps but rather to our living God!

The Seventh Day:
Morning

Christmas for the Sorrowful (1)

The people who walked in darkness
Have seen a great light;
Those who dwelt in the land of the shadow of death,
Upon them a light has shined.
Isaiah 9:2
Read Isaiah 9:1-7

There can be no question about the identity of the member of the "Ful" family being entertained here. Here we have the people of God entertaining none other than Sorrowful. The words "gloom" and "distressed" (v. 1) tell us as much.

What was the cause of this sorrow? The Assyrians had inflicted great distress on the northernmost tribes of Israel, Zebulun and Naphtali, and they were now hovering menacingly over the remaining portion of the kingdom of Israel and over the kingdom of Judah. So the people of Zebulun and Napthali were already living in deep darkness (v.2), and the dark storm clouds were gathering for many others.

It is possible that the words of the passage before us were sent by Isaiah to the distressed northern tribes to comfort them. The other possibility is Isaiah delivered this message to his own people, the people of Judah, to assure them of a glorious future that would include even those northern regions now under Assyrian control.

This much is beyond dispute: the message of Isaiah found its ultimate fulfillment in the Lord Jesus Christ. We know this because when Jesus began His ministry in the northernmost region of Israel, Matthew claimed it as a fulfillment of Isaiah's prophecy (Matt. 4:12-16).

We can say, therefore, that through the words of this passage the prophet Isaiah was comforting the sorrowful people of his day by pointing them ahead to the coming Christ. In essence he was saying: "You must look beyond the sorrow of this time to the coming of the one who can drive sorrow away."

We are also living in an age of sorrow. Millions know what it is to have the dark clouds of gloom hovering over them. Why are so many sorrowful today? "Gloom-makers" abound. Sickness, death, financial hardship, family tensions—all of these and many more generate sorrow. Sorrow is not, however, the only thing that connects us with Isaiah's distant day. Just as he pointed his sorrowing people to the Christ, so we can point the gloomy of our day to Christ. The only difference is that while Isaiah pointed to a coming Christ, we are able to point to the Christ who has come.

How does Christ drive sorrow away from human hearts? The prophet gives us the answer to that question by calling our attention to the four names by which the coming Christ would be known: Wonderful Counselor, Mighty God, Everlasting Father, and Prince of Peace.

What balm and solace there is for the sorrowing in those four names! They affirm that each sorrowing child of God has four things in Christ that can drive sorrow away.

A Wonderful Counselor to Guide

First, we have a wonderful counselor to guide us. When sorrow wraps us in its gloomy embrace, we feel the need for someone to come alongside us to comfort and guide us. And there are all kinds of counselors who are eager to do so. The psychics tell us to call their hotline. The psychiatrist tells us to join his therapy group. Newspaper columnists tell us to write them a letter.

While there is an abundance of counselors today, there is no counselor like the Lord Jesus Christ. He is in a class by himself. When sorrow strolls down life's pathway and knocks at our door, He is there to understand and to offer sympathy and guidance.

Where do we find the guidance Christ offers? It's right there in the Word of God, the Bible.

The psalmist says as much. He knew what it was to have difficulty and sorrow, and in the midst of that sorrow he opened his Bible and began to read. And his testimony is that he found help and guidance there. He says to the Lord: "Your word is a lamp to my feet and a light to my path" (Ps. 119:105).

The author of Proverbs also knew about the sorrows of life, and he knew what it was to find comfort and guidance in the Word of God. He says: "For the commandment is a lamp, and the law a light" (Prov. 6:23).

If these men, the psalmist and the author of Proverbs, could walk with us as we walk with sorrow, they would say: "Pick up your Bible and begin to read."

What exactly do we find when we open our Bibles and begin to read? For one thing we find the sorrows of life are not meaningless and pointless, that our heavenly Father has our best interests at heart and is using our difficulties and sorrows to that end. We also find that He is with us in the midst of those sorrows to strengthen and help us. And we are told that we will find relief from our sorrows if we will come to the house of God for worship and to the throne of God in prayer.

But, wonderful as this counsel is, it will not help us if we do not read it and heed it. Those who do so invariably find the gloom of life dissipating and the light of hope and peace breaking through. What a cheering thing it is to have Christ's counsel us through His Word.

To Think About

- We must both read and heed the Word of God. It's relatively easy to understand the message of the Bible, but also dangerously possible not to live in light of what it says to us.

- God gives us the means of grace—specific things we can do to receive His help. They include regularly meeting with His people in fellowship, attending a place of worship where the Bible is faithfully preached and applied, and taking time routinely in prayer. As Christmas approaches, think about how you may make the most of these kinds of opportunities.

The Seventh Day:
Evening

Christmas for the Sorrowful (2)

For unto us a Child is born,
Unto us a Son is given;
And the government will be upon His shoulder.
And His name will be called
Wonderful, Counselor, Mighty God,
Everlasting Father, Prince of Peace.
Of the increase of His government and peace
There will be no end,
Upon the throne of David and over His kingdom,
To order it and establish it with judgment and justice
From that time forward, even forever.
The zeal of the LORD of hosts will perform this.
Isaiah 9:6-7
Read Isaiah 9:1-7

A Mighty Warrior to Defend

There is more to think about in this remarkable passage. When we sorrow, we also have a mighty warrior to deliver and defend us. Here we look at the term "Mighty God." That word "mighty" is often used in Scripture in connection with warfare, and the people of God were accustomed to hearing their God described as a mighty warrior (Ps. 24:8; Zeph. 3:17).

The root of all our sorrows is sin. Yes, sin is the cause of it all. Do our hearts ache over sickness and death? Sin is the reason. Are our families torn with strife and dissension? Sin is the explanation. Are we gloomy over the condition of our nation? Sin is the cause.

Take any problem that comes to mind, and you can finally trace it back to sin. All sorrow and gloom are rooted in the soil of sin.

If Christ is the one who drives sorrow away, He must of necessity be more powerful than sin. This title, Mighty God, assures us that He is.

Here is what we celebrate at Christmas: He who is God by nature took our humanity to himself. Why did He do this? It was so He could go to Calvary's cross and die there. And why was it necessary for Him to die on that cross? It was so He could deliver His people from their sin and all the sorrow that sin produces.

While the power of sin has in one sense been broken in the lives of those who have cast themselves on the redeeming work of Christ, there is in another sense more work to be done. Sin still clings to the people of God in this life, but, glorious thought, there is coming a day when our Mighty God will destroy every last vestige of it. On that day, there will at last be "no more death, nor sorrow, nor crying" (Rev. 21:4).

An Everlasting Father to Care

Next, we have a Father to everlastingly care for us. It is an unspeakable blessing to know our Christ is the Wonderful Counselor who has the wisdom to comfort and guide us. It is also a blessed thing to realize that He is the Mighty God, the warrior-king who has the power to finally remove all sorrow.

While we rejoice in these things, we have to admit that

counselors and warriors today are not people to whom we feel especially close. There is always an element of detachment and distance there.

But all that goes right out the window with the title "Everlasting Father." Here the prophet takes us to a much higher level, to the level of intimacy and closeness by affirming that Christ is like a Father. In other words, He tenderly cares for us as a father cares for the needs of his children. He has a paternal, caring disposition.

Just as no earthly father can detect the sorrow of one of his children without being touched and moved by it, so Christ is touched and moved by our sorrow. And just as caring earthly fathers draw their sorrowing children to themselves for comfort, so Christ draws His people close to Himself in many ways.

A Peaceable Prince to Give Peace

Finally, we have a peaceable prince to give us peace. The kings with whom the people of Judah were familiar seemed to take delight in the bloody agonies of war, but the hallmark of the kingly reign of Christ is peace. He, and He alone, can cause us to be at peace with God and at peace with others.

He has the ability to instill peace within the hearts of His people. On the night before He was crucified, He said to His disciples: "Peace I leave with you, my peace I give to you; not as the world gives do I give to you. Let not your heart be troubled, neither let it be afraid" (John 14:27).

No matter how severe their trials and profound their sorrow, Christians can enjoy peace and tranquility. They can do so because they know that they have peace with

God through the redeeming work of the Lord Jesus Christ, and even life's most ferocious storms can never change that. Further, Christians know that the peace they now enjoy with God will eventually usher them into an eternity in which no storms will ever rage again. Having peace with God creates peace within, and peace within has a marvelous way of softening the sorrows of life.

To Think About

- If you are sorrowing today, look to Christ, the Mighty God, who alone has the power to defeat the thing that causes sorrow, that is, sin.

- How much greater is the everlasting care of Christ than the brief and limited care of an earthly father.

- Peace with God—what a wonderful gospel blessing. Are you at peace with the Prince of Peace?

Christmas for the Sinful (1)

O LORD, I will praise You;
Though You were angry with me,
Your anger is turned away, and You comfort me.
Behold, God is my salvation,
I will trust and not be afraid.
Isaiah 12:1,2
Read Isaiah 12:1-6

Each Christmas we hear countless statements on what Christmas is "all about." Someone invariably says Christmas is "all about" family or sharing or loving or giving or partying and so on.

When was the last time you heard someone say Christmas is all about sin? No one ever says that, but that's exactly what Christmas is about. If there had been no sin, there would have been no need for Christ to come, and if Christ had not come, there would be no Christmas.

The prophecy of Isaiah contains what some scholars refer to as the "Book of Immanuel." This small book begins with chapter seven and concludes with this twelfth chapter. This is a chapter about deliverance. Some think it describes nothing more than the joy the people of Judah would feel when they were finally delivered from the threat of conquest by the Assyrians.

While there can be no doubt that this hymn of praise was indeed a fitting response to that deliverance, we must go beyond it to the far greater deliverance that Christ came to provide. We have a scriptural precedent for doing this. The deliverance of the nation of Israel from Egypt, for instance, is used by the apostle Paul as a type or picture of the Christian's deliverance from sin (1 Cor. 5:7).

In addition to that we must remember we are in the "Book of Immanuel," in which the prophet looks beyond the political situation of the day to that time when God would come to dwell among His people through His Son, Jesus. No mere political deliverance can begin to compare with the deliverance Jesus came to provide for His people.

Each Christian can, therefore, look back on his or her salvation and say to the Lord the very same things that the prophet here records. First, the Christian can truthfully say to the Lord, "You were angry with me" (v.1).

God's Anger against Sin

Nothing agitates folk more than for someone to suggest that God is capable of anger. An angry God makes them angry! As far as they are concerned, anger is beneath God and unworthy of Him.

But nothing is more emphasized in Scripture than the wrath of God. The psalmist David writes: "God is a just judge, and God is angry with the wicked every day" (Ps. 7:11).

David was not alone in teaching this. John the Baptist emphasized it (Matt. 3:12), as did the author of Hebrews (Heb. 10:27; 12:25-29), James (James 5:9), and the apostles

Peter (1 Peter 4:17-18; 2 Peter 2:4-9) and Paul (Rom. 1:18-19; 2:5; 3:5; 4:15; 12:19; Eph. 2:3; 5:6; 1 Thess. 1:9-10).

The book of Revelation also stresses the theme of God's wrath (Rev. 6:16-17; 11:18; 14:10,19; 15:1,7; 16:1,19; 19:15; 20:11-15; 21:8; 22:11,15).

And, most surprising to many these days, the Lord Jesus himself constantly warned about the wrath of God (Matt. 7:13-14; 22:13-14; 23:33; 25:30,41,46; Mark 9:42-49; Luke 16:19-31).

What is the cause of God's wrath? Our sin. Why is God angry with our sin? He is holy. No matter where we look in the Bible we find God's holiness being stressed. Look here in the Old Testament, and you will find this prophet Isaiah having a vision in which the seraphim around God's throne cry: "Holy, holy, holy" (Isa. 6:3). Look in the New Testament, and you will find four living creatures around the throne of God ceaselessly crying: "Holy, holy, holy" (Rev. 4:8).

It's one thing to know God is holy but quite another to know what that means. It means God takes sin with utmost seriousness. He has a settled indignation against it and is set on judging it. It further means that God is absolutely committed to keeping all sin out of heaven. The apostle John writes of the heavenly city: "… there shall by no means enter it anything that defiles …" (Rev. 21:27).

These words caused one poet to write:

There is a city bright;
Closed are its gate to sin:
Nought that defileth,

Nought that defileth,
Can ever enter in.

Christians are people who have realized all this. They, just like everyone else, came into this world with a sinful nature (Eph. 2:1), but, by the grace of God, have come to understand something of the holy nature of God and how sin is an affront to Him. Christians are those who have also realized that they must someday stand before this holy God, and the thought of standing there in their sins overwhelmed them with despair until they found peace with God by turning away from sin and trusting in the appointed Savior.

To Think About

- It's not popular to speak about people today as being sinners, and under the wrath of God, and yet it is a key teaching of Scripture.

- In the New Testament, Paul delighted in the fact that Jesus came into this world to save sinners—of whom he, Paul, considered himself to be the chief. If the "chief of sinners" can be saved, that's surely an encouragement to any other sinner to come in repentance and faith to Jesus! Consider the next reading here to find out more about how God's anger is taken away from sin.

The Eighth Day:
Evening

Christmas for the Sinful (2)

… she will bring forth a Son, and you shall call His name JESUS,
for He will save His people from their sins.
Matthew 1:21

God's Anger Turned Away

It is a glorious truth that Christians can speak of the anger of God in the past tense. They can say with Isaiah: "You were angry with me" (12:1). They no longer have to say: "You are angry with me." For Christians, the storm of God's wrath has subsided and died. It is past, and now they are able to say to the Lord: "Your anger is turned away, and you comfort me" (v.1).

What a gloriously wonderful testimony! Here is the picture. Here is the sinner in his sins, and, because of that sin, the wrath of God is heading toward him. But before that wrath finally reaches him, something steps in between the sinner and God and deflects that wrath.

We have a perfect picture of all this in the story of Noah and the ark. The people of Noah's day were also under the wrath of God. On that occasion God expressed His wrath by sending a flood upon the earth. That rain of God's wrath fell upon everyone except Noah and his family. It didn't fall on them because they were in the ark God had told them to prepare. The rain fell on that ark but not on them. That ark came between them and the wrath of God.

Now let's stop to think about Christmas again. An angel of the Lord delivered this message to Joseph regarding what was about to happen with Mary: "… she will bring forth a Son, and you shall call His name JESUS, for He will save His people from their sins" (Matt. 1:21).

An angel sounded that same theme on the night the Lord Jesus was born. To the shepherds outside Bethlehem, he said: "Do not be afraid, for behold, I bring you good tidings of great joy which will be to all people. For there is born to you this day in the city of David a Savior, who is Christ the Lord" (Luke 2:10-11).

Christ came to save His people, *the people given to Him by the Father in eternity past,* from sin! This is what these angelic announcements emphasized. And what did Christ do to actually provide salvation from sin? His taking our humanity by being born to Mary in Bethlehem, marvelous as it was, did not provide salvation. The importance of Bethlehem lies here: it was the first step on the earthly path that led Jesus to the cross. On that cross the Lord Jesus Christ did for sinners exactly the same thing that ark did for Noah and his family. On that cross the wrath of God fell on Jesus, and since it fell on Him there is no wrath left for all those who are in Him.

The apostle John gets at this truth by calling Jesus "the propitiation for our sins" (1 John 2:2). By using that word, John is telling us that Jesus appeased the wrath of God against sinners. He absorbed it in their stead. The great message of the Bible and of Christmas is this: God's wrath is either upon us or upon Christ. If God finds our sin upon us, He will send His wrath to fall upon us; but if He finds our sin upon Christ, His wrath against us will be turned away.

The Christian is in Christ, and, therefore, can say the wrath of God has been "turned away" from him. Because of that, the Christian can also use yet another phrase from Isaiah 12: "O LORD, I will praise You" (v. 1).

The Christian's Response

Consider again the central truths of the Bible. It tells us we are all in sin and justly under the condemnation of God, but it also tells us that this God has, in grace, provided a way for our sins to be forgiven. That way is His Son. Through Him we are not only forgiven of our sins but are actually adopted into the family of God. As part of God's family we receive innumerable privileges and blessings in this life, and when this life is over, we have the promise that we will be escorted into the incomprehensible and matchless glories of heaven.

In light of all this, it would seem that it would never be necessary to urge those who know Christ to praise the Lord. But it is necessary. As we peruse the pages of Scripture we find the writers frequently urging the people of God to praise the Lord.

To Think About

• Prayer and proclamation: What does it mean to praise Him? Look back at the twelfth chapter of Isaiah again and note the emphasis on using the voice. We are to use it in prayer. The speaker urges us to "call upon His name" (v.4), which probably refers to praising God in prayer. We are to praise the Lord by proclaiming His name to others. We are to "declare His deeds among the peoples" and to "make mention that His name is exalted" (v.4).

• Singing and shouting: We are to praise the Lord by singing (v.5) and by crying out and shouting (v.6). The crying out and shouting refer to expressing joy by making a clear and loud sound. What better way is there to do this than with a good solid "Amen!" in the public worship of the church?

• Christmas reminds us that we have much reason to praise God. A Savior has come! We don't have to remain in our sins and under God's wrath. We can be delivered. Those who have received Christ have been delivered. This is what Christmas is all about.

The Ninth Day:
Morning

This King Is a Stranger (1)

That was the true Light which gives light to every man com-
ing into the world. He was in the world, and the world was
made through Him, and the world did not know Him. He
came to His own and His own did not receive Him. But as
many as received Him, to them He gave the right to become
children of God, to those who believe in His name: who were
born, not of blood, nor of the will of the flesh, nor of the will of
man, but of God.
John 1:9-13

Christmas is the time when Christians celebrate the birth of the greatest king of all times, Jesus Christ. When we think of kings certain things quite naturally come to mind. We think, for instance, of someone who has absolute authority over a distinct group of people. This person is enormously rich, and he indulges himself to the fullest with extravagant living. (We still hear advertisements of products that will help us to live like a king.) This person is always surrounded with servants who answer to his beck and call. Quite often, we think of a king as someone who wields his authority without much rhyme or reason and without the slightest regard to the welfare of his subjects.

As we examine the kingship of Jesus during this Christmas season, we are going to discover He is noth-

ing at all like the typical king. In today's readings, I call
your attention to Jesus as a stranger. Perhaps you have
never thought of Him in this way. The hymn-writer,
Mary MacDonald, thought of it and wrote:

Child in the manger, Infant of Mary
Outcast and stranger, Lord of all.

The Scriptures above reveal two distinct ways in which
Jesus may be regarded as a stranger.

Defying Expectations

Jesus was a stranger to His own people in the sense that
He defied their expectations.

The Jews were certainly looking for a king. Make no
mistake about that. They knew their Scriptures, and
those Scriptures were steeped with prophecies about a
coming king. The Book of Deuteronomy assured them
that a prophet like Moses would arise (Deut. 18:15,18).
King David, their favorite king, had been given marvelous promises that a great king would arise from his descendants (2 Sam. 7:12-13,16). Their prophets had punc-
tuated their prophecies with promises of the coming of
this king, and with intoxicating descriptions of the glory
He would bring to Israel (e.g. Amos 9:11-15; Hag. 2:8;
Zech. 14:1-21).

The people longed for this king to come. The glory
days of Israel had now faded into the distant past and
not even one prophet had arisen in the last four hundred
years to trumpet afresh the promise. We might interpret
this combination of events to mean the people were
ready to give up all hope, but it seemed to cause many of

them to cling more tenaciously to the promises and yearn more intensely for them to be fulfilled.

Right Timing?

More than that, the people believed the time was right for their king to come. As the New Testament era dawned they found themselves buckling under the heavy, iron heel of the Roman Empire. If their king was waiting for the best possible moment to show himself, this would seem to qualify.

One would think such circumstances would have caused them to be very responsive to the ministry of the Lord Jesus Christ, especially in light of the fact that it clearly had the signature of the supernatural upon it. But they were not in the least bit receptive. In the words of the apostle John: "He came to His own, and His own did not receive Him" (John 1:11). Irony of ironies! He is the one who made the world (John 1:3). He is the one who gives the light of reason and conscience to every man in the world (John 1:9). He is the one of whom ample witness was born by John the Baptist (John 1:6-8). He is the one who came not just to the world in general but to His own, the very people that had been the recipients of all the promises. And with it all, He was rejected and crucified!

How could such a thing happen? The answer is Jesus did not live up to the preconceived notions about what their king would be like. They expected Him to burst upon the scene, start gathering followers by making blistering speeches against the Romans and all the other Gentile "dogs," use His supernatural powers to throw off their bondage, and take Israel to a level that would surpass their golden age under David and Solomon.

How differently, in the wisdom and purpose of God, matters would work out...

To Think About

▶   God's ways are so different than our ways! Who would ever have expected the Messiah to come in such a humble and unassuming way?

▶   The king became an ordinary person, just like we are (though without sin); what an encouragement that is to us to draw near to Him, trusting Him to help us in our need!

This King Is a Stranger (2)

*For such a High Priest was fitting for us, who is holy, harm-
less, undefiled, separate from sinners, and has become higher
than the heavens; who does not need daily, as those high
priests, to offer up sacrifices, first for His own sins and then
for the people's, for this He did once for all when He offered up
Himself.*
Hebrews 7:26-27

When Jesus came on our earthly scene, He did so by
making an attack—and it was an attack not on the
Romans (and the injustices they had perpetrated on the
Jews), but an attack on the sins of His very own people.
He blistered them instead of the Romans! He had the
audacity to say they needed to repent of their sins and
accept Him as their Lord and Savior. He added what
seemed like insult to injury by saying His kingdom was
never intended to be of this world, but it was to be a
spiritual kingdom that would be established in the
hearts of all those who truly follow Him.

For a while the people gave Him space to re-think His
position, come to His senses, and make a mid-course
correction, but when it finally became apparent that He
was dead-set on this spiritual business, they consented
to the crucifixion planned for Him by the religious lead-
ers.

And when it was all over they probably went back to their homes, shook their heads over the day's events and muttered: "What a strange one that Jesus was!"

Strange or Different?

When we say someone is strange we usually mean he or she is in some way different from ourselves. We all have the tendency to think we are the normal ones. So it was with these people. They thought they were the normal ones and Jesus was the strange one. So they rejected Him.

But we are incorrect if we conclude from this that Jesus was a stranger only so far as the Jews were concerned. He was and is a stranger to all of us by nature because we are defiled by sin, but He wasn't. This is what Joseph Cook had in mind when he wrote:

Gentle Mary laid her Child, lowly in a manger;
There He lay, the undefiled, to the world a stranger.

This is the truth brought home to us by the author of Hebrews. Jesus, he says, was "holy, harmless, undefiled, separate from sinners" (Heb. 7:26).

We hear so much at this time of the year about Jesus becoming one of us, that we leap to the conclusion that He was just exactly like us. We may even feel the temptation to excuse sin, by telling ourselves that since Jesus became one of us, He understands. The author of Hebrews makes it clear that Christ can sympathize with us because He "was in all points tempted as we are" but he adds that Christ was "without sin" (Heb. 4:15).

We must always remember that Jesus became like us,

but not totally like us. Yes, let's take comfort from the fact that because He became one of us, He understands the human experience. But let's take even more comfort from the fact that He became one of us so He could do something for us, namely, provide the redemption we could not provide for ourselves.

This truth is forcefully driven home in several Scriptures. The apostle John declares: "And you know that He was manifested to take away our sins, and in Him there is no sin" (1 John 3:5). And Paul says Christ, even though He knew no sin, was "made sin for us, that we might become the righteousness of God in Him" (2 Cor. 5:21).

This much ought to be clear to each and every one of us: Jesus could not have provided redemption for us if He had received the same sinful nature we have. Now we are in a position to see why the virgin birth of Christ was necessary. Jesus Christ had to become a man in order to save us. But at the same time He had to be different from us. If He had not been born of a virgin, He would have been just like us. He would have been a sinner himself thus wholly unable to help us.

In short, the only way we could be saved is through one who was fully God and fully man. We needed someone to identify with us and represent us without becoming a sinner himself. This Jesus did.

To Think About

- When the angel appeared to Joseph, he asked him to embrace a baby that was not his own, to embrace this strange baby who was supernaturally conceived. Here is a similar question to you. Have you received this one who was a stranger to His own and a stranger to sin as the King of your life? That is the great question this Christmas message confronts us with.

- Here's the marvelous thing—if you will bow before Jesus in repentance and faith and own Him as your rightful sovereign, you will find He is no longer a stranger but the most wonderful friend you could ever know. This Christmas season will go down as the greatest in your life if you will make it your time to embrace the King of Kings as your personal King.

The Tenth Day:

Morning

This King Is a Servant! (1)

A disciple is not above his teacher, nor a servant above his master. It is enough for a disciple that he be like his teacher, and a servant like his master.
Matthew 10:24-25

It is not too far-fetched to imagine a king who is a stranger to the people over whom he rules. But who can conceive of a king being a servant? It's like talking about a giant pygmy or a square circle. The two simply don't belong together. Everyone knows kings are not to serve, but are to be served.

Jesus Christ is not a typical king, and the Bible makes it clear He came to be a servant. He said it Himself: "... the Son of Man did not come to be served, but to serve..." (Matt. 20:28).

How can such a thing be? Jesus is such a great king that the Scriptures actually call Him "King of kings" (1 Tim. 6:15). If He is the greatest of all kings, how can He be a servant?

Let's stop and think about servants for a moment. What pops into your mind when you hear that word? Do you not think of someone who has work to do? Do you not think of someone who is under authority and who has no will of his own, but simply does the work assigned to him? Do you not think of someone who has

little or none of the world's goods, lives in lowly circumstances, and has no status? Do you not picture someone
whose life involves suffering, pain, and sorrow?

Do you agree these are the major characteristics of the
servant? You will find that all of the characteristics of a
servant are prominently displayed in King Jesus.

Some Servant Characteristics of Jesus

He had work to do

Does the servant have work assigned? So did Jesus. He
did not come to this earth just "to get away from it all"
for a little while. He did not come here because He was
bored with the glories of heaven. He was not in need of a
holiday. He came here because a work had been assigned to Him, the work of redemption.

The Bible tells us that God the Father, God the Son,
and God the Holy Spirit, before the world began, agreed
with each other on this work of redemption. God knew
people would fall into sin, and His heart of grace compelled Him to plan a way to redeem them. The center-
piece of this plan was that God the Son, in the fullness of
time, would leave the glories of heaven, and become a
man Himself. As a man He was to live in perfect obedience to the law of God, and He was to receive the death
penalty that rightfully belonged to guilty sinners. By His
life, He was to provide the righteousness we do not
have; and by His death He was to receive the penalty
our sins deserved. The child of God, then, is one who
has no penalty left to pay because Jesus paid it, and one
who can stand faultless before a holy God because he is

clothed in the righteousness provided by Christ's perfect life.

This is the great work of redemption, and this is what brought the Lord Jesus Christ into this world. And this is why Jesus said He had to come to serve and "to give His life a ransom for many." He came to do the work He had been assigned.

And just as the servant has no will of his own so it was with Jesus. In John's Gospel we constantly find Jesus saying He had not come to do His own will, but the will of the Father who sent Him (John 4:34; 5:30; 6:38; 12:49-50; 14:10).

To Think About

- Can you imagine a servant deciding to go fishing because he didn't feel like working? The idea is ludicrous! Servants don't obey at their leisure and according to their pleasure. The master's will is their will.

- We should be thankful that it was the same with Jesus. He had the servant's mentality, the mentality that bowed to authority, and He refused to depart from the work that had been given Him. If it were not for this, we would have no salvation.

The Tenth Day:
Evening

This King Is a Servant! (2)

*Let this mind be in you which was also in Christ Jesus, who,
being in the form of God, did not consider it robbery to be
equal with God, but made Himself of no reputation, taking the
form of a bondservant...*
Philippians 2:5–7
Read Philippians 2:5–11

More Servant Characteristics of Jesus

Poverty and lowliness

Just as the servant is characterized by poverty and low-liness so was Jesus. He was not born in the capital, Jerusalem, but in tiny Bethlehem (Micah 5:2). He was not born in a palace, but in a stable. He was not surrounded by servants, but by animals. He was not attended by royal physicians, but only by humble parents. He was not greeted by other kings and princes, but only by crude shepherds.

And this lowly beginning was not just an unfortunate episode that was quickly corrected. It was the first installment of His whole life. From Bethlehem's stable He went to Nazareth's carpenter shop, and from that humble shop He went into a ministry in which He had no place to lay His head.

Suffering

Just as the servant's life is filled with suffering and sorrow so it was with Jesus. He knew that pain and anguish of rejection. He saw the havoc created by sin and His sensitive spirit agonized over it. Scripture tells us He wept over the city of Jerusalem (Luke 19:41), and that He was troubled, groaned in His spirit, and wept at the tomb of Lazarus (John 11:33, 35). It also mentions Him sighing (Mark 7:34). The sufferings of His short life finally peaked in the terrible agony of the worst kind of all deaths, the death on the cross.

All of these sufferings fulfilled the prophecy of Isaiah that He would be "a man of sorrows and acquainted with grief" (Isa. 53:3).

In other words, Jesus' servanthood was not mere pretense. It was not a sham but real in every aspect. If He came to do the work of a servant, He had to be a servant in every respect.

Did the King of Glory stoop so low as to become a servant? What mystery! And did He do this so guilty sinners could be forgiven? What mercy! Charles Wesley captured both the mystery and the mercy of the servant Christ performing the work of redemption:

> *'Tis mystery all! The Immortal dies!*
> *Who can explain His strange design?*
> *In vain the first-born seraph tries*
> *To sound the depths of love divine!*
> *'Tis mercy all! Let earth adore,*
> *Let angel minds inquire no more.*

Being Like Jesus—Being a Servant

Jesus' purpose in calling His servanthood to the attention of His disciples was to indelibly etch on their minds that they were to be like Him. His words couldn't be clearer: "A disciple is not above his teacher, nor a servant above his master" (Matt. 10:24). And Paul's purpose in calling the servanthood of Jesus to the attention of the Philippians was so he could say: "Let this mind be in you..." (Phil. 2:5).

Work to do

What does it mean to us that Jesus was a servant? If there was work for Him to do then there must be work for us, His servants, to do. He has provided the work of redemption and there is nothing we can do to add to that, but we do have the responsibility to share the good news of what He has done. And if Christ's servanthood required Him to have no will of His own but to live completely for the Father's will, we who claim to be His servants must learn to submit to His authority.

Lifestyle Adjustments

Do we dare go to the next step? The servanthood of Jesus caused Him to be deprived of the world's goods and live in lowly circumstances. Does this also apply to us? The Bible commands us to live simply and not ostentatiously. It instructs us to avoid making the accumulation of worldly goods our priority, and to support our Lord's work by giving sacrificially from the wealth we have. Jesus himself said we are not to lay up treasures on earth but rather in heaven (Matt. 6:19-21). On another occasion He said: "Beware of covetousness: for a man's life consists not in the abundance of things which he possesses" (Luke 12:15). And Paul added this word: "And having food and clothing, with these we shall be content" (1 Tim. 6:8).

Sharing in His Suffering

Finally, just as Jesus' servanthood involved suffering, so will our service to Him. Jesus said: "Remember the word that I said to you, 'a servant is not greater than his master.' If they persecuted Me, they will also persecute you" (John 15:20). Serve the Lord, and sooner or later you will encounter misunderstanding, ridicule and scorn. It is part and parcel of being His servant.

To Think About

▶ What is our response to these things? Can we truthfully say we are working for the One who did so much work for us? Do we feel a great debt of gratitude for the whole work of redemption? Do we think in terms of being servants?

▶ Christmas is the best of all times for giving ourselves afresh to service, because servanthood is right at the heart of Christmas. This Christmas let's thank God for sending our Servant-King, Jesus, and let's pledge ourselves to follow in His steps.

This King Is a Shepherd (1)

O Zion, You who bring good tidings,
Get up into the high mountain;
O Jerusalem, You who bring good tidings,
Lift up your voice with strength,
Lift it up, be not afraid;
Say to the cities of Judah, "Behold your God!"
Behold, the Lord GOD shall come with a strong hand,
And His arm shall rule for Him;
Behold, His reward is with Him,
And His work before Him.
He will feed His flock like a shepherd;
He will gather the lambs with His arm,
And carry them in His bosom,
And gently lead those who are with young.
Isaiah 40:9–11

Have you ever wondered why the angels announced the birth of Jesus to shepherds? It seems that the birth of the King of kings should have been announced to royalty rather than to ordinary shepherds. Did the angels misunderstand their assignment? Was there some sort of computer foul-up in heaven? No, there was no mistake. God had the birth of the King of kings announced to shepherds because it was appropriate. Jesus was to be a king, but He was also to be a shepherd.

King and shepherd? It sounds like a glaring contradiction. Consider the shepherd of the Bible. First, his life was one of extreme hardship. He was constantly exposed to the extremes of heat and cold. He usually subsisted on meager supplies. At times his life was imperiled as he defended his sheep from the attacks of wild beasts.

His life was also one of dull routine. Each morning he led the flock from the fold to the pasture by going before them and calling to them. At the pasture, he maintained careful watch over the sheep. If one strayed he sought it out and brought it back. He counted the sheep as they entered the fold to make sure none was missing. Since there was usually no door to the sheepfold, the shepherd himself would serve as the door by positioning himself at the opening of the sheepfold. No sheep could leave and no intruder could enter without the shepherd knowing about it.

That's certainly a far cry from the life of a king. The king knew nothing about extreme hardship and dull routine. He was surrounded by scores of people whose sole purpose was to keep him from facing even minor inconveniences. And when the king got bored, there were numerous avenues he could take to find a diversion. The king could travel, throw a party, or call in the court jester.

It seems, in light of these things, to be utterly ludicrous to mention a king and a shepherd in the same breath, let alone suggest one person could be both. But this is, in fact, what the passages in these two readings tell us about Jesus. He is both shepherd and king, the shepherd-king. In other words, He is the king who rules in the manner of a shepherd. He combines a king's authority with a shepherd's heart.

Christ's Coming

This shepherd's heart is what brought him to this world in the first place. We need to frequently remind ourselves that He did not have to come. Sometimes we forget this. We slip easily into thinking He came because He saw something in us. The truth is He came not because of anything in us but rather because of His own heart of grace. The apostle Paul put it like this: "For when we were still without strength, in due time Christ died for the ungodly. . . . But God demonstrates His own love toward us, in that while we were still sinners Christ died for us" (Rom. 5:6,8).

Paul also wrote to the Corinthians: "For you know the grace of our Lord Jesus Christ, that though He was rich, yet for your sakes He became poor, that you through His poverty might become rich" (2 Cor. 8:9).

Realization and Appreciation

Our enjoyment of the Christmas season will increase immeasurably the moment we realize the Lord Jesus didn't have to lift one finger to save us. We were not even worth saving, but He still came. Why did He do it? It was His shepherd's heart. While our Lord was engaged in His earthly ministry He looked upon the multitudes, and "He was moved with compassion for them because they were weary and scattered like sheep having no shepherd" (Matt. 9:36).

That could equally well have been said of the Lord Jesus before He ever stepped into this world. He saw us ruined by sin and facing eternal destruction, and He came. It would have been impressive if Jesus had been so moved by our dilemma that He came down to observe it and to participate in it. But here is how great His shepherd's heart is: He came not just to experience our dilemma but to do something about it. He actually went so far as to die on the cross for guilty sinners. This is how we became His sheep. He purchased us with His own precious blood! (1 Peter 1:18-19). He had a covenant or agreement with God before the world began that He would go to the cross and receive in His own body the penalty our sins so richly deserve. It is through what the author of Hebrews calls "the blood of the everlasting covenant" (Heb. 13:20) that we have our sins forgiven and enjoy peace with God.

To Think About

- Consider God's great care for sinners—so great that, in His eternal counsel, even before the world began, He purposed to show grace and mercy to undeserving people such as we are!

- Jesus himself said: "I am the good shepherd. The good shepherd gives His life for the sheep" (John 10:11). Don't let the glitter of our Christmas observances obscure His shepherd's heart that brought Him, not just to be with us, but to die for us.

The Eleventh Day:
Evening

This King Is a Shepherd (2)

My sheep hear My voice, and I know them, and they follow Me. And I give them eternal life, and they shall never perish; neither shall anyone snatch them out of My hand. My Father, who has given them to Me, is greater than all; and no one is able to snatch them out of My Father's hand. I and My Father are one.
John 10:27–30

Christ's Care as a Shepherd

It is this same shepherd's heart that causes the Lord Jesus Christ to watch over us and care for us. Several things are involved in caring for sheep.

Feeding the sheep: The most obvious task is to make sure they have something to eat. Our Lord's shepherdly care has caused Him to provide abundant food for us. What is the food for His sheep? It is the Word of God. Through this Word we grow into full maturity as His sheep.

Have you ever stopped to ponder the marvelous provisions your shepherd has made for your spiritual nourishment? Churches, pastors, teachers, books—all have been put in place by the shepherd for His sheep. What a shame that we have so many scrawny sheep in the midst of such abundance!

Bringing back the straying: Another aspect of the shepherd's care is to bring back those who are straying. Sheep do have a tendency to stray. If you are one of the Lord's sheep, you do not need anyone to tell you this. You know it all too well because you constantly feel it in your heart. Here, straying sheep, is your consolation: your shepherd will not allow you to stray so far that you are forever lost. The Lord has never lost a sheep and He never will (John 10:27-30). When you stray He will come after you, find you, and restore you to the flock.

The flipside of this is if you stray and the shepherd never restores you, it is because you were not one of His sheep to begin with (1 John 2:19).

Protecting the sheep: Still another aspect of our Lord's care as a shepherd is that He protects us from danger. Yes, sheep have enemies. David, in the process of caring for his sheep, had to kill both bears and lions (1 Sam. 17:34-37). Our enemies, however, are more ferocious and fearsome than mere bears and lions. We are up against Satan himself, the lusts of the flesh, and the constant pull of the world. Sometimes we feel our enemies are too great for us and we begin to lose heart, but the Bible assures us that our shepherd has never lost a battle and we may rest assured that He will see us safely home to our heavenly fold. There no enemy will be able to touch us. Paul tells us the last enemy to be destroyed will be death itself, all will be brought into complete subjection to Christ and God will be "all in all" (1 Cor. 15:26-28).

All of this leads me to a final consideration, namely, the shepherd heart of our Lord causes His sheep to follow Him.

Christ's Effectiveness as a Shepherd

This brings me to the danger of turning the Bible's "wills" into "shoulds." We read these passages about the Lord being the shepherd of His people, and, in light of them, we say we "should" follow Him. But Jesus said something quite different: "My sheep hear My voice, and I know them, and they follow Me" (John 10:27).

There's no exhortation in those words. Jesus was making a flat affirmation that His sheep will follow Him. Yes, sheep stray, but temporarily straying is quite different from not following the shepherd at all. Those who claim to have the Lord as their shepherd and yet do not have the inclination to follow Him are proclaiming that they really do not know the shepherd at all.

What a joy it is to have ruling over us as king One who is really a shepherd at heart! His shepherd's heart caused Him to come and give His life for His sheep. His shepherd's heart causes Him to faithfully and tenderly care for us. Once we see these truths we will find ourselves longing to follow Him. No sheep ever had a better shepherd!

We began this devotion thinking about how appropriate it was for Jesus' birth to be announced to shepherds. Do you remember what these shepherds did after hearing these marvelous tidings? Luke tells us they went to Bethlehem to see the new shepherd. After they drank in the sight, the Bible tells us they did two things: they made it "widely known" that this shepherd had been born and they returned to their flocks "glorifying and praising God." (Luke 2:17,20).

All the Lord's people should celebrate the birth of Jesus in exactly the same way those men did: telling the good news and praising God for the good news.

To Think About

- The words of a hymn express praise to Christ in these words: "Hail to the Lord's anointed, Great David's greater Son!" Think of the wonder of Jesus in His humanity as a descendent of David, the shepherd king, and think of how much greater a King He is!

- Think of the privilege it is to be a sheep of the Great Shepherd. What are you doing to encourage others, friends, family members, colleagues at work, to come to this Shepherd King in a relationship of trust and obedience?

Behold the King at Christmas (1)

*Now after Jesus was born in Bethlehem of Judea in the days of
Herod the king, behold, wise men from the East came to Jeru-
salem, saying, "Where is He who has been born King of the
Jews? For we have seen His star in the East and have come to
worship Him."*
Matthew 2:1,2
Also read Luke 1:31–33

The baby lying in Bethlehem's manger on that first
Christmas so long ago was none other than the King
of kings and the Lord of lords.

We must say this because the angel Gabriel said it to
Mary in no uncertain terms (Luke 1:31-33). The wise
men, who journeyed far to find Jesus, made it clear that
they were searching for the King of the Jews (Matt. 2:2).
Did they have a complete and accurate understanding of
Jesus' kingship? Probably not. But the Holy Spirit of God
had given them enough illumination to know that Jesus
was born not only to be a king but a very special kind of
king.

The gifts they brought to Him speak volumes. There
was frankincense, myrrh and gold. Strange gifts for a
baby you say? Not for this baby! Frankincense (pure
incense) was something offered to God. Myrrh was a
burial spice. And gold was a gift appropriate for a king.

Did they wrap their gifts? No. But wrapped in their gifts was a ton of truth. They had found the baby who was God in human flesh, the baby who had come to this earth in our humanity to die for sinners; they had found the baby who was King over all. Origen was surely correct in saying of the gifts the wise men gave Jesus: "… gold, as to a king; myrrh, as to one who was mortal; and incense, as to God."

The very fact that the wise men worshiped Jesus tells us a great deal. No ordinary baby, this baby! No ordinary king, this king!

But we haven't gone far enough if we merely assert the kingship of Jesus. We must ask: What kind of king? Herod saw in the baby of whom the magi spoke a rival to his own throne. If Jesus had been born a king, He must be the same kind of king as Herod himself—the king of a temporal realm. Herod could conceive of no greater king than an earthly king and no greater kingdom than an earthly kingdom, yet he could not possibly have been more mistaken. Yes, Jesus was a king, but not at all like Herod! Jesus did not come to be mere the temporary king of a temporary kingdom. And He certainly did not come to rule His subjects with the cruelty and heartlessness that was Herod's.

One day, Jesus himself would say to Pilate: "You say rightly that I am a king. For this cause I was born, and for this cause I have come into the world, that I should bear witness to the truth. Everyone who is of the truth hears My voice"(John 18:37).

Three words should spring to our minds when we think of King Jesus and His kingdom: spiritual, universal, eternal.

Spiritual? Yes! Jesus sets His kingdom up in the hearts of His people by freeing those hearts from the dark kingdom of Satan. Jesus enlightens the minds of sinners to understand the truth about their sins and about His redeeming work on the cross. He enflames their affections so they no longer love sin but rather love Him. He enlivens their dead wills so they can receive Him as their Lord and Savior.

Universal: That brings us to the word "universal." Jesus' kingdom is destined to be universally known. If often looks now as if the kingship of Jesus is going to come to nought. Evil is advancing so aggressively and rapidly. Christianity seems to be losing whatever influence it once had. Satan is ever eager and glad to prompt his followers to heap scorn and ridicule upon Jesus. The invisible king of an invisible kingdom! It seems to be absurd. But both will soon become very visible and plain. The invisible king is going to return with the clouds of heaven, and "every eye will see Him" (Rev. 1:7). Then the laughter and mockery will come to a screeching halt, and every knee will bow before King Jesus and every tongue will confess that He is Lord of all (Phil. 2:9-11).

Eternal: Then there is that word "eternal." Jesus' kingdom will last forever (Luke 1:33). Kingdoms here come and go. Kingdoms that once were hailed as being invincible have come tumbling down and turned to ashes. It will not be so with the kingdom of Jesus. His kingdom will completely fulfill the prophecy of Daniel 2:44: "And in the days of these kings the God of heaven will set up a kingdom which shall never be destroyed; and the kingdom shall not be left to other people; it shall break in pieces and consume all these kingdoms, and it shall stand forever."

We never adequately celebrate Christmas if we do not celebrate the kingship of Jesus, taking as our own the words of Charles Wesley:

Born Thy people to deliver,
Born a child, and yet a King,
Born to reign in us forever,
Now Thy gracious kingdom bring.
By Thine own eternal Spirit
Rule in all our hearts alone;
By Thine all-sufficient merit
Raise us to Thy glorious throne.

To Think About

- Jesus is King! A person once quipped well, "He's either Lord of all, or not lord at all."

- The Kingdom of Christ is an everlasting Kingdom. Are you a member of it? Entrance is open to all who will call upon Him as Lord, for it is written in Romans 10:13 "Whoever calls upon the name of the Lord shall be saved."

The Twelfth Day:
Evening

Behold the King at Christmas (2)

For God so loved the world that He gave His only begotten
Son, that whoever believes in Him should not perish but have
everlasting life.
He who believes in the Son has everlasting life; and he who
does not believe the Son shall not see life, but the wrath of God
abides on him.
John 3:16, 36

What should our response be to King Jesus? That depends. It depends on which of two categories we are in, and, by the way, all of the human race falls into one or the other of these categories. In the kingdom of God, there is no distinction between rich and poor, educated and uneducated, Republican or Democrat. As far as the kingdom of God is concerned, we are either believers in the Lord Jesus or unbelievers. We might say we are either submitters to King Jesus or non-submitters. There is no middle ground.

The Response of Unbelievers
What does the Bible say to those who have not submitted to the King? It very plainly tells us that we must repent of our sins and trust in the Lord Jesus. In other words, the Bible calls all unbelievers to repentance and faith.

Repentance: What is repentance? Perhaps the best definition is found here:

I thought about my ways, And turned my feet to Your testimonies (Ps. 119:59).

Repentance is thinking again and turning. So many people these days are so very sure of themselves when it comes to the Lord Jesus Christ. They are so very quick to dismiss Him and to decide that they do not want Him ruling over them. Repentance means we stop dismissing Jesus. We think again about Him. We come to understand our sins and the judgment those sins deserve. We come to understand that Jesus is the only hope for sinners. We come to a radically different conclusion about Jesus, and we turn to Him. Instead of turning away from Him, we do an about face. Instead of offering our backs to Jesus, we turn toward Him.

Faith: Saving faith is not merely knowing the facts about Jesus or even just agreeing with those facts. It is committing ourselves to Christ as the only one who can save us from our sins and the eternal condemnation they deserve. It is resting our hope for forgiveness entirely on what the Lord Jesus Christ did for sinners in His life and death.

Here is how faith speaks: Did the Lord Jesus live a life of perfect obedience to God? Did He live the life that I have refused to live? Then I will not trust in my own good works or any righteousness that I can produce, but I will take as mine the righteousness that Jesus has produced for sinners. Did the Lord Jesus go to the cross to receive the wrath of God in the place of sinners? Then I will take what He did on that cross as my own so I will never have to face that wrath myself.

The Response of Believers

How should believers in Christ respond to His kingship over them? We should do as the wise men did, namely, worship the Lord Jesus.

Worship: What is worship? It is ascribing worth, excellence or value to the Lord. Believers should do this every single day of their lives. Yes, every day ought to be "Worship Day" for the Christian. And while the Lord delights in the private worship of His people, He delights even more in their public worship. Psalm 87:2 says that "The LORD loves the gates of Zion more than all the dwellings of Jacob." The phrase "gates of Zion" refers to a public place, while the phrase "the dwellings of Jacob" refers to private places. So here we have the Lord putting the public over the private in this psalm of worship.

Three phrases come to mind to guide us in this matter of public worship: *show up, think out, tune in.* To *show up* means we go to public worship. Our King Jesus demands this (Heb. 10:25). To *think out* means we ponder deeply what the Lord Jesus has done for us. This is fuel in the tank of worship. To *tune in* means we do not allow our minds to be miles away while our bodies are perched on a pew.

Pay more earnest heed: The author of Hebrews called his readers to pay "more earnest heed" to the things they had heard (Heb. 2:1). We surely do no wrong if we apply his words to how we best respond to our King.

At Christmastime we celebrate His coming to this earth in our humanity. We might say Christmas is the celebration of the greatest person traveling the greatest distance to do the greatest thing. The greatest person is our King, Jesus. The greatest distance is the distance from heaven to a lowly stable in lowly Bethlehem. The greatest thing? The author of Hebrews gives us the answer in four words—"so great a salvation" (Heb. 2:3). Yes, Jesus came to this earth to provide sinners with a great salvation.

To Think About

- As believers, we are at risk of allowing our familiarity with these things to rob us of the sense of awe and wonder that we should have. So we must "pay more earnest heed" to what it means that Christ became a man. We must pay more attention to our King and the salvation He came to provide.

- The letter to the Hebrews tells us very plainly that the option ever before us is either to "pay more earnest heed" or to "drift away" (Heb. 2:1). We are either seriously heeding Christ our King or we are slipping. The professing church today is in great danger at this point. This Christmas, let's make it our business to earnestly worship and serve our King so we never slip.

Afterword

The first line of one of the verses cited in the preceding pages is:

Pause, my soul! Adore and wonder!

Those words put before us our great duty and our glorious privilege each Christmas season. It is to "adore and wonder." To wonder is to feel a sense of admiration and amazement.

It is wonder that we are so apt to miss at Christmastime. I'm sure that the vast majority of those who have read these chapters have been very familiar with the Christmas message for a very long time. We only need to think of the many people who have little or no understanding of the Christmas message to realize how very blessed we are to be so familiar with it.

But our familiarity can also be a serious obstacle for us. Before we know it, we can be numbly going through another Christmas without savoring the wonder and glory of it. If we're not careful, we can find ourselves focusing on being amused instead of amazed.

What are we to do if we have lost the wonder that is so central to Christmas? The author of the line above tells us. It is obvious that he was talking to himself or coaching himself, and this is what we must do with Christmas. We must tell ourselves to think deeply about what we are celebrating and to truly appreciate it.

If the devotions I have offered in this book help each reader to do those things, I will feel very blessed.

About the Author

Roger Ellsworth is a retired pastor, still active in ministry, who lives in Jackson, Tennessee. He and his wife, Sylvia, love the message of Christmas and enjoy sharing the Christmas season with their sons, Tim and Marty, daughters-in-law, Sarah and Rebekah, and five grandchildren, Daniel, Emmalee, Noah, Isaiah, and Eramin.

Roger has written numerous books on the Christian faith, and has exercised a preaching ministry for over fifty years. His sermons are available to listen for free on SermonAudio.com.

Customizable Editions

Did you enjoy reading this devotional book? It is available in a range of special editions from www.twelvedaysofchristmas.net with the choice of different covers and Bible versions cited, and is able to be customized according to the wishes of the buyer. Special discounted prices are available for churches, associations, and ministries. Be sure to visit the site to find out all about these special offers!

www.greatwriting.org
www.twelvedaysofchristmas.net